W9-ALM-075

The Science of Water

LIVING SCIENCE

Janice Parker

Gareth Stevens Publishing
MILWAUKEE

For a free color catalog describing Gareth Stevens' list of high-quality books and multimedia programs, call 1-800-542-2595 (USA) or 1-800-461-9120 (Canada). Gareth Stevens Publishing's Fax: (414) 225-0377.

Library of Congress Cataloging-in-Publication Data

Parker, Janice.
The science of water / by Janice Parker.
p. cm. — (Living science)
Includes index.
Summary: Presents information about the properties, behavior, and uses of water, covering such topics as its various forms, the water cycle, and salt water versus fresh water.
ISBN 0-8368-2469-5 (lib. bdg.)
1. Water — Juvenile literature. [1. Water.] I. Title. II. Series: Living science (Milwaukee, Wis.)
GB662.3.P37 1999
551.48 — dc21 99-28909

This edition first published in 1999 by
Gareth Stevens Publishing
1555 North RiverCenter Drive, Suite 201
Milwaukee, WI 53212 USA

Project Co-ordinator: Samantha McCrory
Series Editor: Leslie Strudwick
Copy Editor: Rennay Craats
Design: Warren Clark
Cover Design: Carole Knox
Layout: Lucinda Cage
Gareth Stevens Editor: Patricia Lantier-Sampon

Photograph Credits:
Chase Day Images: page 12; Corel Corporation: cover (center), pages 4, 5, 7, 8, 9 top, 10, 11, 13 top, 14, 15, 19 bottom, 21 top, 22, 25 bottom, 26, 30; Ivy Images: pages 17 top (Bill Ivy), 17 bottom (Bill Ivy), 20 (Ottmar Bierwagen), 21 bottom (Bill Ivy), 29 top (Bill Ivy), 29 bottom (B. Bachmann/Spectrum Stock), 31 (Tony Makepeace/Spectrum Stock); PhotoDisc: cover (background); Tom Stack & Associates: pages 6 (Novastock), 9 bottom (Doug Sokell), 13 bottom (Ncar/Tsado), 16 (Brian Parker), 18 (Tom & Therisa Stack), 19 top (Tom & Therisa Stack), 24 (John Gerlach), 25 top (Brian Parker), 27 (Inga Spence), 28 (Tom Stack); J.D. Taylor: page 23.

Printed in Canada

1 2 3 4 5 6 7 8 9 03 02 01 00 99

Contents

What Do You Know about Water?

Most of Earth's surface is covered with water. This explains why photographs of Earth taken from outer space make the planet look blue. Water collects and moves in oceans, rivers, and lakes. It falls in the form of rain and snow. Clouds, frost, and dew are all made of water. Arctic glaciers are also made of water. Some sources of water are hidden beneath the earth. Most of the water we drink comes from deep underground.

Water is part of every living thing. Our bodies are full of water. Plants, including fruits and vegetables, are made up mostly of water. Everything in nature needs water to survive.

The first kayaks were made by Inuit people so they could fish and hunt in the water. Today, kayaks are used mainly for recreation.

Puzzler

Think of all the ways you use water every day.

Answer:
Here are just a few ways you may use water:

- to bathe
- to brush your teeth
- to cook food
- to drink
- to flush the toilet
- to skate on or swim in

Bodies of Water

Human bodies are made up mostly of water. We must drink water every day to stay healthy. **Saliva** in our mouth moistens the food we eat before it reaches our stomach. Blood, which is made up mostly of water, carries **oxygen** and **nutrients** throughout our bodies.

Human bodies constantly lose water through **perspiration**. When we perspire, or sweat, water is released from our skin. This helps cool the body down if we get too hot. Sweating provides temperature control for our bodies.

If the body loses too much water, we feel thirsty. Thirst is our body's way of telling us to drink more water. Water helps all parts of the body work well. If we do not drink enough water, we will become sick.

Camels need only a little water to live. They can go for several days without drinking any water.

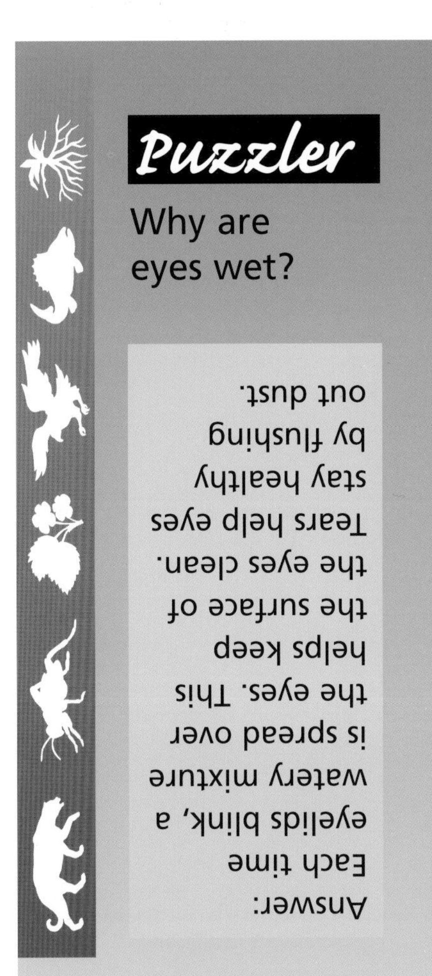

Puzzler

Why are eyes wet?

Answer: Each time eyelids blink, a watery mixture is spread over the eyes. This helps keep the surface of the eyes clean. Tears help eyes stay healthy by flushing out dust.

The Water Cycle

Like plants and animals, water has a life cycle. Water is always changing. It is constantly being recycled.

The water cycle includes the clouds in the sky. Water from the clouds falls to Earth as snow or rain. It then moves through rivers and streams. Water often returns to the air as **water vapor** or clouds, and the cycle begins again.

Water never disappears completely. It may seep into the ground or flow into a river. Water that looks like it is not moving, such as lake water, is changing. If the air is dry and warm, water turns into water vapor and rises into the air. This is called **evaporation**. Evaporated water in the air cools down and forms water droplets. These droplets form clouds.

When clouds become too heavy with water, the droplets fall to Earth as rain. If the air is cold enough, water falls as snow.

Raindrops vary in size, speed, and shape. Large raindrops fall faster and are flatter than small raindrops.

Puzzler

Where does rain go once it hits the ground?

Answer:
Rain seeps into the earth, or it collects and flows into rivers or lakes. Some rain will evaporate back into the air.

Water, Ice, and Steam

Pure water is colorless. It has no taste or smell. Water that has color, taste, or smell contains other things. Water comes in three forms: liquid, solid, and gas. Liquid water is what we usually think of as water. We drink it, bathe in it, and feel it as rain.

When liquid water is heated to 212° Fahrenheit (100° Celsius), it changes to a gas. We call this **steam**. When liquid water is cooled to less than 32°F (0°C), it changes to a solid. Ice is solid water that is made up of many water crystals.

Activity

Exploring Ice and Steam

Pour some water into a pot. Ask an adult to heat the water on the stove. Watch the water as it gets hotter. Small and then large bubbles will begin to rise to the surface. When the water bubbles rapidly, you will see steam rising from the pot. This water is very hot. Be sure not to touch it.

Pour some more water into an ice cube tray. Place the tray in the freezer. Look at the tray every hour or so. What happens to the water?

Clouds, Rain, and Snow

Millions of tiny water droplets or ice crystals make clouds. As a cloud cools, water droplets join other droplets. When the droplets are heavy enough, they begin to fall to the ground as rain. If the air is cold, raindrops freeze as they fall to the ground. Frozen rain is called hail.

Hard hailstones slightly larger than these shattered this windshield.

Snow is different from hail. Snowflakes are made of tiny ice crystals. Snow forms in clouds that are very high and cold. Freshly fallen snow is light and airy. If you melt 4 inches (10 centimeters) of snow, it makes only 1/3 inch (1 cm) of water.

Activity

Measuring Rainfall

Listen to a weather forecast. If it is going to rain, place a glass container with a large opening outside. Put a funnel in it. Rain will collect in the container. After one day, measure the amount of water inside the container. This is the amount of rainfall in your area for that day.

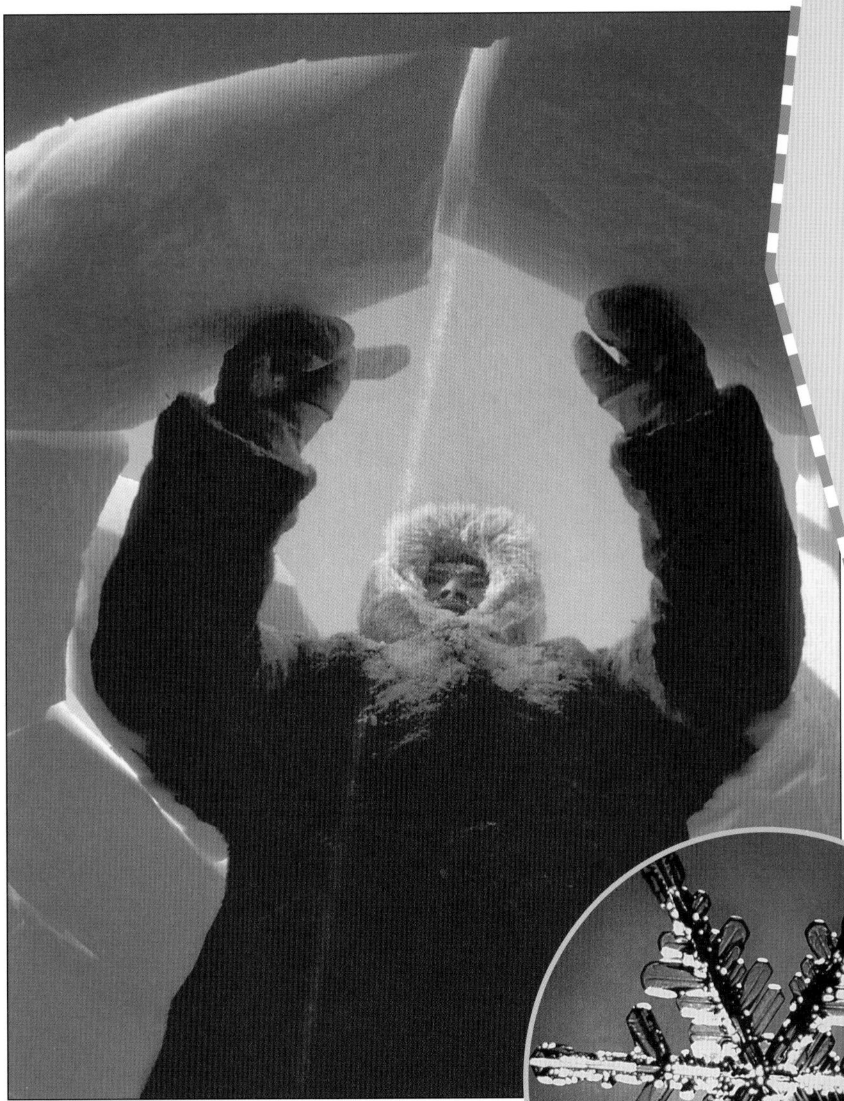

No two snowflakes are exactly alike, but they all have six sides.

Snow can be used to build a house. Blocks of snow are stacked on top of one another to make an igloo.

Freezing and Boiling

Ice is frozen water. Water freezes when its temperature is colder than 32°F (0°C). As water freezes, it expands, or gets bigger. Ice is made up of many tiny ice crystals.

Penguins spend their days on the ice and swimming in the cold ocean water.

Water turns into steam when it is boiled. This means it is heated to the **boiling point**. The boiling point of water is usually 212°F (100°C), but this can differ, depending on where you live. The higher you live above **sea level**, the higher the boiling point.

In some parts of New Zealand, steam from the ground is used to produce electricity.

Activity

Expanding Water

Pour some water into a plastic container with a lid. Place the lid on and leave some air in the container. With a felt pen or a piece of tape, mark the water level on the container. Place the container in the freezer for a few hours. Look at the container once the water has turned to ice. Is the ice at the same level as the water was?

Wet and Dry

Water makes things wet. To stay dry, we wear clothes that are waterproof. Liquid runs off waterproof items, such as raincoats and umbrellas. Ice is dry. A cloth will not get wet if there is ice sitting on it. When the ice starts to melt and turn to liquid, the cloth will get wet.

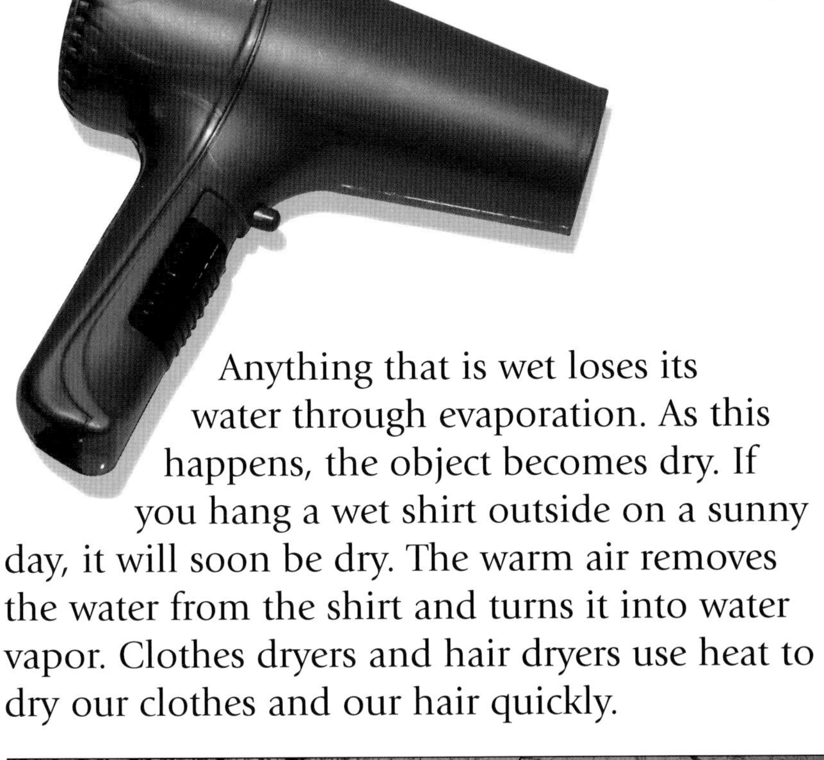

Anything that is wet loses its water through evaporation. As this happens, the object becomes dry. If you hang a wet shirt outside on a sunny day, it will soon be dry. The warm air removes the water from the shirt and turns it into water vapor. Clothes dryers and hair dryers use heat to dry our clothes and our hair quickly.

Puzzler

On a warm, sunny day, spray or pour some water on concrete outside. Pour half the water in a sunny area, and half in a shady area. Which do you think will evaporate more quickly? Why?

Answer: The air in the sunny area will be warmer than the air in the shade. The water in the sun will evaporate more quickly because warm air attracts more water vapor.

Working with Water

A marine biologist is a person who studies the plants and animals that live in salt water. Marine biologists learn as much as possible about living things in the sea. They may try to save plants and animals that are **endangered**. Marine biologists sometimes work in science laboratories or aquariums. They often work outdoors, at the seashore or in the oceans. To become a marine biologist, you must go to college or a university and get a degree.

Underwater mini-submarines are used to explore and study ocean life.

Some meteorologists give weather forecasts on television.

Activity

Do Your Own Research

Many people work with water in their jobs. Ask a parent or teacher to help you find out more about these careers:

- deep sea diver
- lifeguard
- meteorologist
- plumber
- water scientist (hydrologist)

Water in the Air

The air around us contains water vapor. We cannot see water vapor because it is a gas. Warm air often contains more water than cold air. When warm air cools down, the extra water turns into a liquid and makes larger drops of water. This is called **condensation**.

Dew helps plants grow in places that receive only a little rainfall.

Condensing water usually attaches itself to an object. Water that attaches itself as moisture to grass and plants is called dew. Dew forms when the outside air cools down at night. The next morning, the temperature of the air will warm up again. When this happens, the dew evaporates back into the air.

Puzzler

Water droplets collect on the outside of a glass containing an icy cold drink. Where were these water droplets before?

Answer: The droplets come from water vapor in the warm air surrounding the glass. When the warm, wet air touches the cold glass, water vapor condenses into droplets on the glass.

On the Move

Some water moves very little. Water frozen in large glaciers can stay there for many years. Natural stores of water exist deep underground. Most water moves constantly and flows downward. **Gravity** pulls water toward lower areas. Water melting from the tops of mountains flows downward in creeks and rivers. It keeps moving downhill until it reaches a lake or ocean.

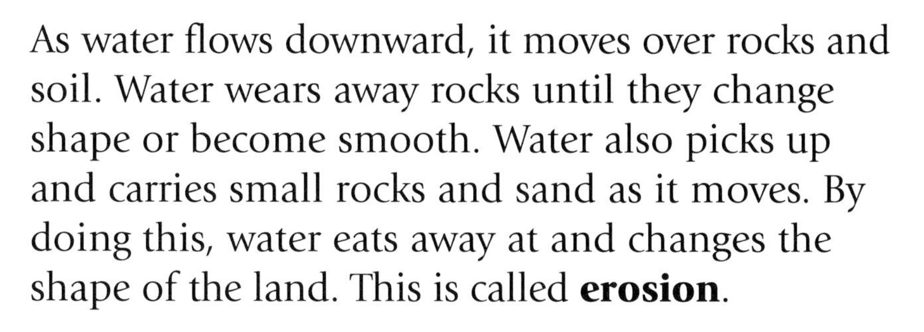

As water flows downward, it moves over rocks and soil. Water wears away rocks until they change shape or become smooth. Water also picks up and carries small rocks and sand as it moves. By doing this, water eats away at and changes the shape of the land. This is called **erosion**.

Water flows upward only if it is being soaked up by an object, such as a sponge. If you place the edge of a sponge or paper towel into water, the water is pulled upward. Plants soak up water in the same way.

The Grand Canyon was formed over millions of years by the Colorado River. The river wore through layers of rock.

Puzzler

Erosion is damaging to land. It carries away good soil that is used to grow crops. How can farmers prevent soil from being carried away by water?

Answer: Farmers can slow down erosion by planting trees, bushes, and grass near the edge of nearby streams or rivers. The roots of these plants help hold the soil in place.

The Power of Water

Flowing water can be very powerful. Many years ago, people thought of a way to use water for power. Water flowing over a waterwheel makes the wheel move. The power that results from this moving wheel can then be used to make other machines work.

Dams are used to trap large amounts of water. By releasing water steadily, the dams produce electricity called **hydroelectricity**. *Hydro* means "water." Many people around the world use hydroelectricity to light their homes and heat their stoves.

The Grand Coulee Dam is the largest concrete dam in North America.

Puzzler

Steam is also used to make machines work. Trains once used steam engines to move. How does a steam engine work?

Answer: Steam takes up much more space than water. When heated water turns into steam, it expands and moves gears in the steam engine. These gears make the train wheels turn.

Salt Water vs. Fresh Water

Most of the water in the world is salt water. It cannot be used for drinking, daily bathing, cooking, or watering farmland. Oceans are made up of salt water. Salt water is different from the fresh water that is in most lakes and rivers. Salt water does not taste good, and it makes us more thirsty. If you water most plants with salty water, they will die. Some plants and animals have **adapted** to live in or around salt water.

The Pacific Ocean is home to numerous plants, fish, and sea mammals. It is the largest and deepest ocean in the world.

Fresh water is good for drinking and watering crops. It is found underground, in lakes and rivers, and in rain. Farms sometimes are located in dry areas, where fresh water is scarce. **Irrigation** is used to water crops in these areas. Irrigation means moving fresh water from a place with plenty of water to dry land. The water is moved through wells or canals.

Activity

Floating Eggs?

It is much easier to swim in ocean water than in lake water. Things float more easily in salty water. Try this experiment to see if this is true.

You will need:

- two glasses
- water
- salt
- a spoon
- two eggs

Pour water into both glasses. Add a few spoonfuls of salt to one glass. Stir the salt until it dissolves into the water. Carefully place an egg into each glass. Does the egg float in both?

Some irrigation systems use sprinklers to spray water onto crops.

Fit to Drink

Not all fresh water is safe to drink. Our drinking water naturally contains minerals and other substances that we cannot see. Many of these substances are good for us. They often make water taste better. But water can also contain things that are dangerous for us to drink. Pollution, chemicals, or bacteria in water can make us sick.

Polluted water can be dangerous.

Cities and towns treat fresh water before it goes into houses. Water treatment plants remove some dangerous substances. Chemicals are often added to water to kill bacteria. In some parts of the world, there is no safe water to drink. Many people get sick and even die from drinking dirty water.

A water filter can be attached to a faucet. It improves the taste of drinking water.

Puzzler

Can you tell if water is safe to drink just by looking at it? Can you tell by smelling or tasting it?

Answer:
No. We cannot see many of the chemicals or bacteria that make water unsafe to drink without using a microscope. Water may look cloudy or dirty. It may smell or taste strange and still be safe to drink.

Saving Water

Only 3 percent of all water in the world is fresh water. Most fresh water is frozen in glaciers and ice caps at the North and South poles. There is a limited amount of fresh, clean water for people to use on Earth. People who live in areas with clean water often use much more than they need. We waste good water or pollute it with garbage or chemicals. One day soon, there may not be enough clean water for people and farms.

Many steps can be taken to protect water and keep it from being wasted. We can help keep our water clean by not making it dirty with pollution. It is important not to waste clean water. We should all try to use only as much water as we need.

Here are some tips to help you save water:

- Make sure the taps in your house do not leak.
- Do not leave the water running while you brush your teeth.
- Try not to spend more than five minutes in the shower. If you prefer baths, fill the tub only half full.
- If you do not finish drinking a glass of plain water, use the rest to water a plant, or put it in a pet's water dish.
- Put barrels or other containers outside to collect rainwater. This water can be used for watering plants inside the house and in the garden.
- If you go camping, never dump dirty or soapy water into a lake, stream, or creek.

Puzzler

How much water can be wasted by one leaky tap?

Answer:
One dripping tap can leak enough water in a year to fill two swimming pools!

Glossary

adapted: having become suited to a certain environment or way of life by changing gradually over a long period of time.

boiling point: the temperature at which water begins to change from a liquid to a gas.

condensation: when water changes from a gas to a liquid.

endangered: when a species of plant or animal is at risk of dying out.

erosion: when water or wind wears down rocks and land and carries away soil.

evaporation: when water changes from liquid to gas.

gravity: the force that pulls objects, including water, downward, toward Earth.

hydroelectricity: electricity that comes from power plants that use water to make power.

Inuit: an Aboriginal people who live mainly in the Canadian Arctic and parts of Alaska.

irrigation: when people move water from one area to a drier area.

kayak: a long, narrow boat with pointed ends, usually made for one person.

nutrients: substances needed by the body and obtained from food.

oxygen: a colorless, odorless gas that is found in water and air.

perspiration: water that comes out of our skin to help cool us off.

recreation: an activity done for fun and amusement.

saliva: a watery liquid in the mouth that moistens food.

sea level: the level of the surface of the sea.

steam: water that has turned into gas after reaching the boiling point.

water vapor: water in the form of a gas.

Index

Web Sites

wwwga.usgs.gov/edu

www.hooverdam.com

www.city.niagarafalls.on.ca

www.dobedobedo.com/ice.htm

Some web sites stay current longer than others. For further web sites, use your search engines to locate the following topics: *hydroelectricity, irrigation, oceans,* and *storms.*